LIBRA
Thru the Numbers

Paul & Valeta Rice

SAMUEL WEISER, INC.
York Beach, Maine 03910

First published in 1983 by
Samuel Weiser, Inc.
P.O. Box 612
York Beach, Maine 03910

Copyright © 1983 by Paul and Valeta Rice

All rights reserved. No part of this book may be reproduced in any form or by any means, without permission in writing from the publisher.

ISBN 0-87728-571-3 (Libra)

Library of Congress Catalog Card Number: 82-63004

Typeset by Deerfield Printing Company
Printed by Mitchell-Shear, Inc.

People wishing to contact the authors may write them at the following address:

Paul and Valeta Rice
F.A.C.E. Association
177 Webster Street, Suite A-105
Monterey, Ca. 93940

Contents

Authors 4
When? 5
Libra 7
How to Compute Your Destiny 9
Destiny Number 1 11
Destiny Number 2 12
Destiny Number 3 13
Destiny Number 4 14
Destiny Number 5 15
Destiny Number 6 16
Destiny Number 7 17
Destiny Number 8 18
Destiny Number 9 19
Destiny Number 11 20
Destiny Number 22 21
Destiny Number 33 22
Destiny Number 44 23
Destiny Number 55 24
Destiny Number 66 25
Your Personal Chart 26
Personal Year 27
Personal Month 27
Table of Personal Months 28
Challenges of Life 33
Table of Challenges 34
Numbers 36
Bibliography 40

AUTHORS

If Valeta and Paul Rice sound familiar, it may be because of their extensive travel to many cities from Fairbanks, Alaska all the way down the coast to San Diego, California, and across the continental United States to Baltimore, Maryland. During their invitational stopovers they conduct workshops and seminars about Name Analysis and Birthdate Analysis, traveling together for over twenty years.

The Rices have been interested in occult studies for over forty years, starting with the receipt of the book on ESP from Duke University. Their search for esoteric knowledge carried them into Astrology, Reincarnation, Palmistry, Tarot, Color, Music, I Ching, ESP, Dream Analysis, the Qabala, Yoga, Structural Dynamics, meditation/visualization/healing and many more sciences. Their Socratic and regression techniques have been rewarding to clients.

While their professions are different (Valeta is a minister and psychic counselor, Paul is a professional engineer), they enjoy the cooperation that team teaching provides. Each summer they travel wherever they are invited to teach Name Analysis and Birthdate Analysis as well as conducting private sessions by appointment.

Their major work, now in its second printing, is concerned with name analysis and is a book called *POTENTIAL!*, which is available at many book stores or can be ordered directly from the authors.

A second work, called *TIMING*, is a book dealing with birthdate analysis for all the birth signs.

WHEN?

When shall I start my next project?
When should I ask for a raise?
When should I sign that contract?
When should I get married?
How will I feel when I retire?

How many times has a person looked for an answer to these questions? During this modern age the veil has been lifted on the ancient science of the vibration of the NUMBERS. This ancient science, known as the *metaphysical science of numerology*, was developed by Pythagoras, who lived in the sixth century B.C.

The simplicity of NUMEROLOGY is astounding. If you can count on your fingers you can use Numerology. It requires only a few hours study before you can begin to put to use the basic facts that you have acquired. This knowledge will give one the opportunity to see himself and other acquaintances in a better light. Apparently its simplicity is the reason Numerology was used less than other occult sciences in the past, and our society today seems to prefer complexity also.

Surprisingly, the knowledge of the numbers which govern your life will reveal many things you already know, that you had suspected or you had hoped were true.

The Numerologist takes his place alongside the Astrologer, Graphologist, Palmist and the Tarot reader, who all believe that we came into this life, not by chance, but by choice, and from these arts or sciences much can be revealed about a person's life.

Numerology reveals the vibrations in many categories including the number connected to the Birth Date, the Personal Year, the Personal Month and how the planet vibrations correlate to these numbers.

The awareness of the numbers connected to these categories helps us with a yearly and monthly course to follow.

Everyone wants to be happy and prosperous. Many unfortunate people have not learned to harmonize their birthdate vibrations with the timing of their decisions.

We are constantly called upon to make decisions which may make significant changes in our lives. Often we make the wrong decisions over family, friends, or in business because our "TIMING" is off.

The simple system of the vibration of the numbers and how they pertain to your life and the timing of your decisions will help you to come to logically deduced insights and, if carefully followed, will make you increasingly happy and prosperous throughout your lifetime.

Pythagoras, who lived twenty-five centuries ago, is considered the Father of Numbers. It is believed that he received his knowledge of the occult value of the numbers while in Egypt and Babylon. He taught these concepts and many more in his School of Occult Philosophy where the few who were allowed to attend learned how "everything can be related to numbers."

The Science of Numerology is not a quick way to happiness and achievement; it is only by becoming aware of your favorable number vibrations and then changing the unfavorable vibrations that you can smooth your pathway.

Numbers live and numbers tell and everyone can become aware of their vibrations and their relationship to themselves through the numbers.

We have explored the mundane and esoteric values of the numbers and their relationship to astrology with a lot of help from our guides.

This knowledge we wish to share with you.

MAHALO!
(Thank you!)

LIBRA

September 22nd to October 22nd CARDINAL/AIR

The SCALES Ruler: VENUS

'Ere LIBRA is weighed in the balance and found wanting, he brings Indian Summer's heat; then wages celestial war with wind and rain, the harbinger of winter. This masculine sign represents the soul turning from the "me" consciousness to "us." Libra is about relationships, sometimes windy and stormy and sometimes warm with passion. He leaps into the air to gain perspective, seeing both sides of the challenge. Libra, the Venus Lover, not wanting to take sides in an argument, the pacifier, "let's reason together."

Golden Libra's color of intelligence shines on friends and enemies alike, though Librans seldom admit to having enemies. They prefer communicating and patching up quarrels after they have perhaps precipitated them.

Good listeners. Good talkers, too. Classed as the beautiful people, handsome men and pretty girls, they smile even when angry.

They are busy, busy people who expend so much energy that you're out of breath just watching them, then they balance vigor with lethargy—doingness with dreaming—and therefore keep body, spirit and mind balanced. They know when to quit and refresh themselves in sleep.

Don't ask your Libra child to move out before he is ready. He likes the security of home and will quickly find another "nest" if forced to leave too early.

This Cardinal/Air sign shows deep emotions, empathizing one time with your problems and the next time not really seeming to care, probably off in some distant fantasy world of his own making.

Librans like the truth, make good lawyers, psychologists, mediators and claim adjusters. Just don't hurry them as they like to examine both sides of the problem before coming to a conscientious decision.

PARTNERS: A Libra lover or mate is an exciting adventure. You are gentle, attentive and intelligent. You prefer quality, harmony, music, poetry and the proper use of words. You take time to make up your mind about the opposite sex—but remember that your ruler is Venus, the planet of love. John Lennon, Marcello Mastroianni, Brigitte Bardot and Charles Boyer are Librans who are all lovers in their unique way.

VENUS: The ruler of love and beauty brings devotion and harmony to any relationship. There is gentleness and courtesy in the Librans who express this powerful love of mankind, lovers, mates, beauty and home. Love can move mountains of indifference and strife. On the negative side Venus can be overly sentimental or even evasive of commitments.

CARDINAL: This is Libra's aspect of force manifesting in matter—fast action, impulsiveness and strong ambitions. Librans act first and argue later. This is creativity on a mental level.

AIR: These are the virtues brought forth from former lifetimes. This is knowledge gathered from experience, study and intuition. Judgement and intelligence balance the scales.

NEGATIVE VIBRATIONS: Beneath all this charm and diplomacy is an iron fist in the velvet glove. When you make up your mind it is difficult to persuade you otherwise, for Libra is a mental sign, the sign of intelligence. You want to be liked by everyone, yet are secretive about personal matters. Can switch sides in an argument but deny indecisiveness.

NUMBERS: The NUMBER that is connected to Libra's BIRTH SIGN increases or decreases Libra's energy. Wherever you find Libra in your chart look at the influence your DESTINY NUMBER has on this house in your horoscope.

HOW TO COMPUTE YOUR DESTINY

Your DESTINY, sometimes called the LIFE PATH, is the road that you as an individual travel. This is why you are here, what you should be doing in this lifetime in order to fulfill your soul. The NUMBER combined with your LIBRA BIRTH SIGN reveals your soul urge, your reason for incarnating this lifetime. If you do not follow your DESTINY, you can become frustrated with unresolved goals.

Each month is represented by a number:

JANUARY	1	APRIL	4	JULY	7	OCTOBER	1
FEBRUARY	2	MAY	5	AUGUST	8	NOVEMBER	2
MARCH	3	JUNE	6	SEPTEMBER	9	DECEMBER	3

Write your BIRTHDATE on your PERSONAL CHART, page 26, using the NAME of your month—SEPTEMBER or OCTOBER—not the number of the month. Be sure to use the full year, *i.e.*, 1935, *NOT* '35; or 1940, *NOT* '40, or whatever is the year of your birth. We use the "1" in the year, *i.e.*, 1935, 1966, 1940, as well as the rest of the numbers.

On scratch paper add the number of the month, the day of the month and the year of your birth together; then reduce this number by constantly adding the numbers together until you come to a single digit or a MASTER NUMBER.

The MASTER NUMBERS are **11, 22, 33, 44, 55** and **66.**

EXAMPLE: Sept. 30, 1947 (1 + 9 + 4 + 7 = 21, 2 + 1 = 3)
              9   3   3 = 15; 1 + 5 = **6**
EXAMPLE: Oct. 16, 1953
             10 16 18 = **44** or **8**
EXAMPLE: Oct. 20, 1969
             10 20 25 = **55** or 10 = 1 + 0 = **1**

Experiment with your birthdate and see if you can come up with a "hidden" MASTER NUMBER.

We call the second and third examples *Research and Discovery* since we have found a *hidden* Master Number. When the Master Numbers are hidden an unexpected talent lies in the direction of the vibration of that particular number.

So, Libra, every time you find a **1, 4, 6** or **8** in your birth sign or someone else's birth sign, try all these methods. Then you find out if you or another person is vibrating on the Master Number or the single digit. There are persons who are content to vibrate and work on the single digit pulsation and put their talents to excellent use in that position rather than try for the esoteric vibration of the Master Numbers. This depends a lot on other numbers which concern several other categories in numerology.

The main purpose of finding your DESTINY NUMBER is to realize where you are in life's stream and learn to flow with it.

The DESTINY NUMBER and your BIRTH SIGN are two things that you cannot change. You were born on a certain day, month, and year, for you chose to be here at that time to experience what you have come to this lifetime to learn.

Another way to research and discover if you have a hidden Master Number is to add this way:

September 24, 1903 = 9 + 24 + 19 + 03 = **55** or **1**
October 20, 1917 = 10 + 20 + 19 + 17 = **66** or **3**
October 17, 1970 = 10 + 17 + 19 + 70 (1 + 9 + 7 + 0) = **44** or **8**

We always show the single digit that the Master Number reduces to—**55/1** or **66/3** or **44/8**—in order to see which level a person vibrates on.

DESTINY NUMBER 1

You have a creative streak with this Destiny Number that shows brilliance, Libra. Your plans and ideas may not agree with the standard societal mores, but they will be wild and wonderful and make you seem like you just arrived from another planet.

Injected into your concept is a sort of logic that is hard to escape and the people around you may look puzzled for a while and then say, "That's a good idea, why didn't I think of that!"

You are the searcher, looking for the truth that is hidden from the public eye; the investigator, the detective, the philosopher who gathers books around him, seeking that nugget of enlightenment. Then you explode into sparks of energy and physical activity, determined to run farther, act better, paint more accurately and rise to the epitome of your talents—NOW! And strangely enough, you do just that. You activate yourself and others.

Here is the creative business man with innovative ideas, the Truman Capote of writers, and you too can write if you try. Put your dreams on paper for others to see.

As a lover or mate, how can you fault that charming smile and soft approach, the tender caring, the flowers and the unexpected gifts so apropos of the occasion or of your innermost desires?

NEGATIVE: Your air sign lets you fly high, Libra, and sometimes it could get lonely up there with your rareified ideas and plans. You might have to go after your ideals by yourself and not let these "authorities" impinge on your visions. Others may try to guide you into thinking "their" way or try to hold you from going forward; watch it.

Number 1

Color: Red—for energy, the cardinal thrust.
Element: Fire—the innovator, the burning desire.
Musical Note: C—the self-starter, self-motion

DESTINY NUMBER 2

As a **2** you become sensitive to the moods of your co-workers and can patiently cooperate with them as you all go about the work-a-day world. You may still retain your ideas and ideals yet you are able to see other peoples' side of the problems that come up each day.

It may be difficult for you to come to an agreement with yourself about what to do regarding decisions, since you balance one opinion against another, seeing clearly how peace can be obtained, yet unwilling to put forth the solution for fear of hurting someone's feelings. Compromise from both sides could be the answer. You are the diplomat, the one who loves to have things run smoothly without chaos or arguments. Men and women sitting down and reasoning together for the good of mankind is your ideal.

Your air sign can catch the butterfly of inspiration, bring it down to the peace table where your cardinal energy ignites the inspiration and passes it on to those who will listen and act.

This consideration and love for others shown by your Venus side will shine on your lover or mate. Select one who realizes that you cannot do your finest work in a messy office or home. You need order and calmness as a **2**.

Your ability as a peacemaker may not bring you great rewards in this lifetime, yet you will know that you smoothed the road so that **1**s, **8**s and the Leos of this world can march in triumph.

NEGATIVE: If you will not listen to other viewpoints then justice cannot be served. Everyone has a right to their day in court to express opinions. Your Libra conscience seeks justice, so listen a little to the other side. Sensitivity about yourself can bar the door to truth.

Number **2**

Color: Orange—for balance and harmony.
Element: Water—dealing with the emotions.
Musical Note: *D*—for harmony and tranquility.

DESTINY NUMBER 3

Your usual happy nature is evident in this number, Libra. There is joy in livingness, eating well, playing hard, and working steadily at and with the things you love to do. Use your charm, Libra, to captivate your guests, entertaining them and spreading good humor.

Communication is the keyword for **3**, and this means listening as well as talking—listening with your inner ear to really hear what a person is saying with his heart.

3 has an interesting combination of the creativeness of **1** and the diplomacy of **2** inherent in the structure of the **3**, this latter number wanting to take these abilities and move them forward into the goals you propose for yourself.

This is the lifetime to socialize, make contacts that will help you in business. Learn to move easily among many different kinds of people. Many **3**s are in the entertainment field as directors, actors, TV executives, commentators, talk show moderators and other places where there is a stage, a microphone and someone to talk to.

Another facet to your nature is being a good counselor because of the communicative factor in **3**. Your bent toward philosophical matters could put you into a religious or metaphysical field, learning about the mysteries of life so you can use them to assist others.

Choose a mate or lover who holds excitement for you. The stolid stay-at-home would conflict with your gregarious nature in the **3**, Libra.

NEGATIVE: The applause of public life could bring on conceit and exaggeration of your abilities. Be a shining light, not a temporary 30-watt bulb. A lower tone **3** would turn to jealousy and intolerance.

Number **3**

Color: Yellow—for expression.
Element: Fire—for energy.
Musical Note: E—for feeling.

DESTINY NUMBER 4

Your devotion to duty is inherent in **4**, Libra. You are appalled at unfair treatment of your co-workers or your superiors. You want justice at any cost. This feeling carries through to your personal relationships to the point where you sacrifice your own goals in order not to hurt someone, like keeping a mate or lover beyond the time when happiness was there. You may postpone decisions on separation from your mate rather than make a clean cut.

Your business ventures will be advanced by your personality. Female Librans make good models and beauticians. Both sexes could succeed as attorneys or politicians. Your professional life will be enhanced by a firm commitment to your mate.

You may be faced with handling property matters and paying attention to smaller business economies. Get your finances in order, cut and prune the deadwood from your company. Unproductive people are such a drain on your monies.

Love is demonstrated by the order, loyalty and quality that you show, Libra. You have no trouble manifesting love and you do show it to others generously. Let those around you see your deep love for mankind also.

NEGATIVE: You could be overcautious in your dealings with others and become withdrawn and rigid in your opinions. Concentration is your keyword so that your organized life can become a reality and not a burden which is formed of chaos. Do one step at a time, on one project at a time, if too many decisions are coming your way.

Number 4

Color: Beautiful, healing green—project this color from your heart.
Element: Earth—the stable person.
Musical Note: F—for construction, building, and making your life mean something.

DESTINY NUMBER 5

Librans are usually interested in the arts. Plays, music, drama, paintings and good books absorb your waking hours. This number gives you a broad viewpoint from which to travel Libra.

Your demand for personal freedom may keep you from listening to ways to plan your life, but that is okay, as you will find your own way. You have many choices—you are the traveler, lighting here and there, the messenger, bringing light and life into any company as you entertain with story, song and anything which will keep the party active.

This restlessness continues even when you reach the top of your profession, for you can see miles ahead of anyone else, into the future.

You could become a terrific writer—novels or books about those places you have visited in fact or in your dreams. Adventure calls and you go, sampling the essence of life, yet you need some roots to go home to.

Libra **5**s are more mental than they realize as they can remember all the things they have seen and things they have learned—and apply them when necessary.

Better team up with someone who can go to strange places with you for companionship; these could be your roots. Carry your love with you like a snail carries its house wherever it goes.

NEGATIVE: Inconsistency is the bane of the **5**s. They can go into a funk and not know what they want, unable to choose a direction, sitting and sulking. This turns into blaming others and indulging in self-pity. Being Librans they soon snap out of it and come back to their sunny selves again. Don't be afraid of changing conditions, flow with them.

Number **5**

Color: Turquoise—like a refreshing breeze.
Element: Air—the breath of life.
Musical Note: G—denoting change.

DESTINY NUMBER 6

This harmonious Destiny Number agrees with your concept of staying healthy, Libra. Work hard, play hard and then collapse for a while. People seeing you lazing around the house when the screens are leaning against a snowbank outside the windows will want to scream at you for wasting your time. Then when you are fully rested you go out, put up the storm windows, put away the screens, shovel coal, clean the walks and then ask your mate for something to do as you are bored. There just doesn't seem to be a happy medium for your moods, Libra.

This number helps keep you equalized, if that is what you want, keeping your scales balanced so that you don't tip one way or another.

Your emotions run high in this number as it is emblematic of the cosmic mother who nurtures all things. You may weep over a dying plant, then throw it out the next day to make room for a new one. This change of character is not quite like the Gemini who becomes a different person from time to time. Librans go deeply into their emotions yet stay the same loving and fair-minded person.

You would make a wonderful parent and a loving mate. Home is where the heart is. Let your Venus love come through to all those around you.

NEGATIVE: If you get anxious about your family you might start telling them what to do. And they don't like it one bit because they will be all different numbers and signs, which could confuse you a lot. Take pride in your mate and family and your business ventures without being prideful. Take care of the small things and the big things will take care of themselves. When you are down you could turn cynical and suspicious of others' actions.

Number 6

Color: Royal blue—for stability. Meditate on this color for balance.
Element: Earth—for responsibility.
Musical Note: A—for receptivity and harmony.

DESTINY NUMBER 7

When we stand at the crossroads—good and evil, right and wrong, or decisions to go this way or that—we need to use the inner wisdom of 7 Libra. Since this is your Destiny Number you can bridge from the known to the unknown by gathering knowledge from books, lectures, meditations, etc. This perfect occult number is called the *eye of the needle*, when we stand at the gateway between mundane and esoteric knowledge.

This number gives you the opportunity to analyze your past successes and mistakes so you can build a secure future. Reverse the mistakes and make them the building blocks for a firm foundation. What is your real purpose this lifetime?

On the esoteric level 7s are the mystics who can heal spiritual gaps in a person's aura. This permits healing of the physical body. Remember that permission must be asked of the person YOU feel needs healing, Libra. A person may prefer to take ownership of his problems instead of understanding what caused them in the first place.

Your mate or lover needs patience to understand your "in-depth" contemplation or mood. This need for quiet is not compatible with responsibility to family unless you have other numbers in your chart that indicate your love for children. You always need roots and someone to come home to, Libra.

NEGATIVE: The temptation is to remain aloof from the cares and tribulations of life, Libra, when you are working on this side of 7. You just don't want to be bothered. Of course, this is no way to increase your knowledge or elevate yourself. You can't be charming all the time, just don't confuse mysticism with aloofness and neglect of your friends.

Number 7

Color: Violet—which stands for reverence.
Element: Water—flowing with your knowledge.
Musical Note: *B*—for reflection on the past.

DESTINY NUMBER 8

"There is a tide in the affairs of men which, taken at the flood, leads on to fortune." (Shakespeare).Your cardinal sign means action, direct and to the point; sometimes it can mean impulsiveness and impatience. **8** is power on the material level for most people, Libra. It means using your energy to attain high positions in government, entertainment or business. Many people of power and wealth will come your way to ease your path toward the fulfilling of your dream of success. Cultivate those who can help you gain your purpose in life, Libra. Think big and reach for the opportunities which can advance your position.

On the esoteric level you can reopen your third eye, turn on your psychic ability to discriminate between fact and fancy. Meditation could bring in the power to see auras and further meditation could teach you how to read the auras.

If you choose the arts you can become famous as an artist, dancer, sculptor, or in any field you choose because you have the grace and rhythm and exhibit this form to the public. It may be a little difficult to believe that you have this kind of talent but when you realize that you can do many things that others cannot, nothing can stop you from accomplishing your goals. You have only to make up your mind (and you have strong mental powers) to act, sing, become head of a corporation, run for public office, etc.

The opposite sex will be drawn to you, attracted by your grace and your success.

NEGATIVE: Jealousy can rear its ugly head as you try to outdo someone else. This seldom works. The best thing to do is just be BETTER! This high-powered Destiny Number has great rewards and great pitfalls. Watch your companions along the way.

Number **8**

Color: Rose—for love.
Element: Earth—for achievement, material gain.
Musical Note: High C—for achievement.

DESTINY NUMBER 9

This compassionate number is suitable to your loving nature, Libra. Many religious leaders have this number as they wish to reduce the suffering of mankind. Your sincere desire to help those less fortunate than you goes beyond your personal desire to serve yourself. Your energies are put to use in social services, or, in one-to-one charitable outpouring of your love and money. You are the one who literally will give the shirt off your back to help a friend.

You love to give expensive presents to your lover or mate, yet these gifts are purchased with deliberation so that the gift fits the recipient and the occasion as well. Such thoughtfulness.

This number also means success and achievement in this lifetime as you finish your tasks. So many people like to begin a project, then get bored and never finish. When you begin something, after much deliberation, you are dedicated to keeping it going or finishing the job, depending on the type of job it is. When a cycle of work is finished there comes a surge of energy to lift your physical and emotional spirit.

9 is a total of all the numbers from **1** to **8**, thus giving **9** the vibrations of all the numbers, with **9** being the finish line.

NEGATIVE: People will drain you of energy if you let them. This drain could turn you from a loving Libra to a selfish, inconsiderate person. Letting others take advantage of your good nature is a form of dissipation, because it makes you feel noble; and this could be habit forming. Assist others with kindness, but don't get bitter if they refuse your friendship at a later date. People hate to be obligated to a friend. Let others do something for you to balance the energies.

Number **9**

Color: Yellow-gold—for perfection, the desire to make everything perfect, even people.
Element: Fire—for warmth, cuddling up to.
Musical Note: High *D*—for accomplishment.

DESTINY NUMBER 11

MASTER NUMBERS carry a higher vibration than the single digits. You'll notice that **11** reduces to a **2**. Check both vibrations to see which level you are on. The **11** is the idealist, the one who wants and must have perfection in all he does. Your idealism lies in a situation where right would be served on both sides of the equation or problem; the scales must balance for you. This balancing would be the interpretation of perfection for you, everyone getting a piece of the pie, everyone being satisfied with the ruling.

You would make a fine judge with this number, a case worker in the social service department and would do well in any job requiring a tempering of decisions. Diplomacy in political situations or settling disputes in the family circle would give you the feeling of a job well done.

Some **11**s want to stay in the background and not share their tact and magnetism with others. Team up with a **22**, Libra, and you will have the dreamer of a perfect world (**11**) with a mate who can bring it into reality (**22**).

Your intuition is extremely well developed. This, combined with your mental agility, and excellence of performance in those professions and hobbies you should choose could send you right to the top of whatever occupation you concentrate on.

NEGATIVE: Here are the fanatics who have turned their need to create a perfect world into an ego trip. They want everyone to join them. If you don't join their society, etc., you are purged from their sight; and that could be a little drastic. Be idealistic without becoming cynical and aimless.

Number **11**

Color: Silver—for attraction.
Element: Air—for the idealist.
Musical Note: High *E*—for magnetism.

DESTINY NUMBER 22

22s discipline body and mind, Libra. You are able to do tremendous feats in sports and in the arena of business where a clear thinking process is required to arrive at a sensible solution. Your direction could take on an international flair, government position, fame in the entertainment world or wherever a master organizer is needed.

22 is universal power on the physical level, a practical level. In order to take advantage of this energy you have to think big, act big, and take control of a situation where leadership is needed. You can be the head of a large corporation, a manager of big business, head of the household or builder of beautiful structures.

In your spiritual life you could be a strong force to bring others into a belief system that is founded on logic and balance—as much right and fairness for both parties as possible; or different systems could be analyzed to bring forward the best points of each one.

Usually this Master Number carries the mark of good health as you are too busy to bother about small complaints and just tell your body to heal itself. It does.

NEGATIVE: You may become discouraged when you are unable to bring a satisfactory conclusion to your huge efforts, Libra, in whatever you decide to do, and then withdraw from society. This monk-like existence is not for you, since you are the lover of the zodiac. Put your loving spirit into high gear again and have another go at it. You really cannot be indifferent to mankind. Be a doer, not a big talker.

Number **22**

Color: Red-gold—for practical wisdom, using the things you have learned for practical application. Element: Water—for cleansing. See reality. Musical Note: High *F*—for physical mastery.

DESTINY NUMBER 33

You are suited to handle artistic lines more than you are for running a business. Your emotional involvement with the beauty of paintings, flowers, nature and all things that have line and color invite your attention, Libra. Words also attract you, which means you would make a good defense lawyer, protecting your clients. Or you would find arguing against the injustices to man a fascinating subject.

Think of **33** as being a combination of the idealist (**11**) who wants to have perfection in all things, and **22**, who sees how this perfection can be accomplished if we do not become embroiled in silly disagreements, Libra.

The human race expresses emotions. The beginning of these emotions are centered in experience and what we remember truthfully about them. How do we react to grief? To loss of love? These reactions color our life today. You may try to rationalize your feelings (balancing the scales) and yet your seeking after the truth brings you face to face with yourself. How honest are you in defining your emotions? Use the Venus love vibrations to love yourself as well as others.

Your reactions to the opposite sex can magnetize them into occupying your space. Your large, beautiful eyes show the emotion you feel in your heart.

NEGATIVE: There is a healing quality in **33**, Libra, that would be turned off if you decide that you do not care about people. Your gifts would be negated and it would be difficult to raise any positive emotions or feelings that would radiate good will. Also, do not work on others' emotions to their detriment; that's bad karma.

Number **33**

Color: Deep sky-blue—for intensity.
Element: Water—for emotional mastery.
Musical Note: High G—for emotional healing.

DESTINY NUMBER 44

You have a keen mental approach to problems, Libra, always weighing pro and con, trying to find the truth. The scales, representative of your sign, can become unbalanced with attachments to one way of life while closing your eyes to other outlets to your personality. There are many paths up the mountain to enlightenment. Total dedication to your life's work is commendable, but leave a little time for the expansion of yourself and your spirit.

We use logic to weigh one idea against another. There is the two-valued logic (right and wrong), the three-valued logic (right, wrong and maybe), and then there is simply your side, my side and the correct side. If we take a quantum leap we get to infinite-valued logic, "righter" at one time than another or "wronger" at one time than another—infinite distance on either side. You have the ability to use one or more of these processes, Libra, as you evaluate your opponent. Your intelligent mind can bring slower thinkers to a decision.

44 is a combination of the idealistic **11** and the **33** which is emotional mastery. This means that the creative, idealistic ideas you have are put forth with emotion (which you can control) and enthusiasm so others help you accomplish your goals, **44**.

44 is also the combination of two **22**s, physical mastery over self. **44** can stand alone as the powerful manifesting number for material goods.

Social service or one of the healing professions would suit your loving nature in this number, Libra.

Select a mate or lover who can give you lots of love and attention and yet can keep up with your quick penetrating intelligence.

NEGATIVE: You could get impatient with a co-worker or your mate is unable to keep up with you physically or mentally or both. Watch confusing values.

Number **44**

Color: Blue-green—for tranquilizing vibes.
Element: Earth—for mental mastery.
Musical Note: High A—for mental healing.

DESTINY NUMBER 55

The love and kindness you show to others is a true expression of **55**, Libra. This life-giving number is the light of creative love being channeled through you and shining forth to those around you. At this level you can bring light and knowledge from higher dimensions into your consciousness, then teach those who are ready to receive these inspiring messages.

Think of **55** as being a combination of **22**, the physical and practical master, and **33**, the master of the emotions. **55** brings these two together with the life essence which means that you can learn to understand how to control the emotions of self or others in a practical way. Look at where you are and where others are when exposed to events that become a problem, Libra. Just take a look at how these events are handled. Do you talk your way out of a situation, rationalizing your feelings or do you look the event squarely in the eye to see the truth? How do others react?

Or you can think of **55** as being the combination of **11**, the idealist, and **44**, the mental master. The idealist provides the creative inspiration that the mental master sets into viable form, then **55** gives life to the project. So you can be creative and practical as you put your project into action (life force).

Your mate or lover cannot help but see this beautiful love that you contain and share.

NEGATIVE: On this side of the number you become the victim of life; working to decrease knowledge, burning books, repressing the ideas of others, refusing promotions to deserving employees, suppressing action toward expansion and invalidating others as well as self.

Number 55

Color: Red-violet—the abundant life energy.
Element: Air—for spirituality. Discover the way of the masters. Meditate on your color.
Musical Note: Chord of G—for spiritual healing.

DESTINY NUMBER 66

Use the Research and Discovery method, page 11, to see if this powerful Master Number is hidden in your birthdate, Libra. **66** is love energy, the full realization that one cannot love others until he loves himself and can outpour this feeling to others.

66 is truly the cosmic mother vibration, the double six leading to the 9: $6 + 6 = 36$; $3 + 6 = 9$, which is brotherly love for all mankind. We are not talking about sex, although that is an important part of lovingness; we are referring to the ecstasy that comes over us sometimes in meditation, giving us the feeling that we are truly connected with the cosmos, the Oneness.

Share your viewpoints with others and teach others how to complete the circle of love. You have a lot of love to give and share, Libra. You could become the counselor, the psychologist, the minister; or you could go into social work or the peace corps.

NEGATIVE: A negative **66** could gather many people into his/her camp by selling them on the idea that "this is the only way to salvation." This **66** would use the love energy to enslave others, make them do things "in love" that go against our moral codes. Another negative vibration is repressing love for self and others, keeping family and friends chained with, "You don't love me any more!"

Number **66**

Color: Ultra-rose—the fullest expression of love on this planet. Meditate on this color, it will fully open your heart chakra if all the other laws are followed which have led you to this initiation.

Element: Fire—for burning away the dross, getting rid of the unwanted attitudes, habits that keep us from progressing, indulgences that cloud our aura.

Musical Note: Any chord struck in harmony.

YOUR PERSONAL CHART

Birthdate _____
Birth Number _____
Birth Sign _____
Birth Element _____

This planetary aspect represents the moral excellence and goodness that the soul has achieved in former lifetimes, virtues which will assist a person in this lifetime.

Birth Musical Note _____

Personal Year for 1983_____
Personal Year for 1984_____
Personal Year for 1985_____
Personal Year for 1986_____
Personal Year for 1987_____
Personal Year for 1988_____
Personal Year for 1989_____
Personal Year for 1990_____

Personal Month Numbers:

January _____   July _____
February _____   August _____
March _____   September _____
April _____   October _____
May _____   November _____
June _____   December _____

Challenges:

Major _____
1st Sub-challenge _____
2nd Sub-challenge _____

PERSONAL YEAR

The PERSONAL YEAR NUMBER is the vibration that influences your life in any given year. This is a fine focus of JUPITER, the planet of benevolence and idealism. Jupiter showers you with all the good things of life as long as you recognize what the good things are. If you are operating on the negative side of Jupiter, it could lead you into extravagance and greediness.

To obtain this number you add your BIRTH MONTH and your BIRTH DAY to the year you are seeking. For example: If your birth date is September 22, 1961, and you want to find the PERSONAL YEAR for 1981 you do this:

Add 9 (September) to 22 (the day) to 1981 = 2012
2012 = 2 + 0 + 1 + 2 = **5**; the PERSONAL YEAR for the year 1981 for the person with the birth date of September 22, 1961.

Do *not* use your own *birth* year; use the year in which you wish to find your PERSONAL YEAR.

PERSONAL MONTH

Still under the influence of that great planet, JUPITER, we also find our own PERSONAL MONTH by adding our PERSONAL YEAR to the current month or the month we are seeking.

Example: September 22, 1961 is the birth *date*. We want to find the PERSONAL MONTH for *October 1981*. Since we have established the PERSONAL YEAR for this birth date for 1981 as **5**, we simply add the month of October (10 = 1) to this number.

5 (Personal Year) + **1** (October) = **6.** Therefore, the PERSONAL MONTH for the birth date of September 22, 1961 is **6** for October 1981.

Compute your PERSONAL MONTHS and find the interpretations on the following pages.

TABLE OF PERSONAL MONTHS

JUPITER: EXPANSION, UNDERSTANDING, FRIENDLINESS, ABUNDANCE, INSPIRATION, INCREASE, SPUR.

The definitive words for Jupiter listed above captured the essence of the positive side of Jupiter's vibrations. Understand these words by using a good dictionary as you discover the true meaning for yourself. Meditating on all the descriptive words given in this booklet will assist you also.

The NEGATIVE side of the JUPITER vibration is:
EXTRAVAGANCE, INDULGENCE, CYNICISM, GREED.

When we talk about the TIMING of your decisions we need to remember that Jupiter has an influence as well as the vibration of the number that you find for your own PERSONAL MONTH. The interpretations for personal months are as follows:

PERSONAL MONTH 1

A new nine-month cycle of endeavor always starts with the number one month. The **9** month is the ending of a cycle. This month you listen to your own counsel, your own desires to succeed. This is the month to start something depending on your Destiny Number. Use the interpretations of our Destiny Number to go along with any and all of the Personal Month interpretations in order to get a better view of where you are and what to do about it, Libra. This month could also bring about a rebirth of ideas you had in the last **9**-month cycle that you dropped for one reason or another. Your creative power stems from your innate sense of justice and fairness, Libra. You can reason in the abstract sense and philosophical manner to arrive at your conclusions. Create your own plans that you want to carry forward and complete in the next nine months. Plan carefully, then put your plans into action. Avoid decisions that depend on emotions. Be factual.

NEGATIVE: Indecision could restrain you from reaching your goals. Arrogance can deprive you from accepting others' viewpoints.

PERSONAL MONTH 2

This is a good month for personal relationships, Libra; show your love and your good nature to the public as well. They usually like to see your smile or grin as you bring sunshine into their lives. This is not the month to start a business, a love affair, etc. That was last month and the month coming. This is the month to grow within a love that you already have, let it ripen. Confront situations that need to be aired and talked over. This is the month for compromise if patience is used with a lavish ladle. Use your intuition to avoid mistakes in judgement. Cooperation with your boss or your employees or co-workers is needed for your advancement in your chosen profession this month.

NEGATIVE: You could lose your patience since you love a good argument, not listening to yourself and what you may say that will hurt another person. If your opponent begins to agree with you, you are apt to change sides and argue for a while there. This is confusing to people and will not bring about compromise.

PERSONAL MONTH 3

Now you can go ahead with your plans and bring success to your ventures. Relax a little and stop arguing about nit picky stuff. You can also indulge yourself a little, take a vacation, have some fun, spread humor and good will wherever you can. You are a good host and entertain your guests with stories, music or whatever is your special talent. This is a strong month combining the creativity of **1** with the diplomacy of **2** to fulfill your dreams of success (**3**). Get out into the country to explore nature, growing things, and the fragrance of clean air (if you can find it). You need to experience the beauty of our planet in the flowers and grasses, hills and valleys, desert and lakes.

NEGATIVE: Your uncertainty disturbs your contentment if your scales get tipped too much.

PERSONAL MONTH 4

If last month was playtime for you, Libra, then you are prepared to get back to the old mill and grind away at your regular duties. **4** is usually called the work number; however, if you like to be involved in your profession, your school or your retirement, then *that* is play for you and **4** holds no restrictive bonds. **4** is also the manifesting number, getting what you want, visualizing it happening and making it appear. You can make it appear faster if you have laid the groundwork in the **1** and **2** personal months. Establish yourself on a firm base for future growth with your lover or mate and your work-a-day world even if you have to give a little.

NEGATIVE: You could express the firm side of your personality to the extent of seeming to be rigid in your opinions, Libra. You like to argue and will take the opposite side of any argument, just don't try to suppress others' opinions. They might even fight back.

PERSONAL MONTH 5

Your adventurous soul goes soaring in this month, Libra, giving you the changing patterns that you like, although they seem to be hard to handle. There are so many choices presented this month that it will be difficult for you to decide which is the better one to take. More than four choices over one challenge could make you struggle for air. Get some time alone and away from the crowd so your decisions about women or men (depending on your sex) can be wisely made. Remember you like cleanliness and beauty and order in your life.

NEGATIVE: You could get very confused over the exciting things that are happening too fast if they imply disharmony. Instead of creative mental level (**5**) you could become sloppy and withdraw into sleep or self-indulge in whatever turns you on. Don't be afraid of change, it brings fresh air.

PERSONAL MONTH 6

This is family month, time to pay attention to your mate or lover, your children (if any), and your brothers and sisters. Use love to promote the harmony you came here to express as a **6**. This is the most harmonious number for you, Libra, as it is the nurturer, the cosmic mother, the one who takes care of people and things. Venus (ruler of your sign) can assist you, through love, to open the doorway to higher mind through harmony and harmonizing your relationships with others. This is not a time to be careless in your work or profession; take meticulous care with details of documents; read the fine print of anything that you have to sign. Do not force issues; ask for guidance as this is a personal time for you. People depend on seeing your charming smile and your radiant personality.

NEGATIVE: You could become picky as your temperament vacillates between being anxious about the outcome of your adventures and the calm, all-knowing part of you that knows everything will be okay. Don't interfere this month in places and spaces where you do not belong. Advice is seldom welcome and those who think they want it, want it least of all.

PERSONAL MONTH 7

"Of science and logic he chatters, as fine and as fast as he can; though I am no judge of such matters, I'm sure he's a talented man," (Winthrop Praed: *The Talented Man*). And we are sure that a **7** month holds much talent for logical deductions, using the magic you have to enchant and disarm the unwary—even wary. Take a look at your successes and your mistakes of the past six months so you can bridge the gulf of indecision. By looking back, you can look forward to plan the next move in your chess game of business or love, for next month is a power month for you, Libra. Be prepared for a good, prosperous month ahead.

NEGATIVE: You could become skeptical of your talents and withdraw into a sulk if things do not go your way.

PERSONAL MONTH 8

Take care of matters pertaining to material growth, money, possessions, business and finance this month, Libra. Now you can reap some of the rewards due from your careful decisions of the previous month. Exercise your charm and ability to weigh in the balance the steps you must take to further your career. You have a good sense of values, knowing what to buy or sell after you have taken the time to ponder the action quietly with no interruptions. If disturbed, you have to start all over again to get your wheels turning.

NEGATIVE: There is a facet to your nature, Libra, that most people do not understand. You cannot be pushed into making a decision if you feel that time is needed. You are not usually intolerant but your impatience will loom large on the horizon if there is friction in the ranks of your co-workers. You could lose money and prestige this month if you make hasty decisions under pressure.

PERSONAL MONTH 9

Time for romance, Libra! Be aware of the opposite sex (as you usually are anyway) for some exciting, albeit brief, episodes may happen this month. **9** is always brotherly love, also taking care of those less fortunate than you. Sometimes just using your smile will change things in the office, for people cannot help reacting to a Venus child with love. Finish as many projects as you can during a **9** month. This number is the tearing down and the terminating of jobs left undone in order to make room for the new and exciting territory still unexplored.

NEGATIVE: Avoid being unkind to people, dogs, cats, birds and inanimate objects. If you play the selfish game you could reap scorn instead of success. Ranting about injustices gets you a good soap box lead, but unless you DO something about it you are only left with a box to burn. When your scales are unbalanced, Libra, you slide into dissipation, abusing your body through overindulgence. The bitterness you feel will change to sweetness when your scales come back into balance through diet, change of environment or change of attitude.

CHALLENGES OF LIFE

CHALLENGES are obstacles we encounter during this lifetime. We are now concerned with the timing of events that stop you from progressing until you understand just what the obstacle is and means.

In the FIRST HALF of your lifetime, you will encounter a SUB or minor challenge which is represented by a number.

In the SECOND HALF of your lifetime, you will encounter a SUB or minor challenge which is represented by a number.

The MAJOR CHALLENGE, also represented by a number, is with you your entire lifetime until you solve the mystery. We accepted these challenges when we decided to incarnate on this planet so that we can strengthen the weak links in our destiny. Recognizing these weak links by finding the negative influences of these numbers will be helpful.

SATURN is the planet known as the DISCIPLINARIAN, the teacher, the door to the initiation and all these good things we shy away from or fear. See Saturn's other side—if you have no game going, no challenge and life proceeds smoothly straight down the road with the same scenery—where is the spice? Understand the good that Saturn brings us. Saturn is connected to the challenges of life.

FIRST SUB CHALLENGE: Subtract the number of your birth MONTH from the number of your birth DAY or vice versa.

SECOND SUB CHALLENGE: Subtract the number of your birth DAY from your reduced birth YEAR or vice versa.

MAJOR CHALLENGE: Subtract the FIRST SUB CHALLENGE from the SECOND SUB CHALLENGE or vice versa. Place all these numbers in your PERSONAL CHART on page 26.

EXAMPLE: September 25, 1954

```
         9     7    1
        ─────────────
            2    6    = 2 is the First Sub-Challenge
               4        6 is the Second Sub-Challenge
                        4 is the Major Challenge
```

TABLE OF CHALLENGES

1—Many people will try to dominate and control your life. The remedy is choosing your own way without being belligerent about it. Know when you are right and please yourself after considering all the facts. Strengthen your self-determinism and be the daring, creative person you really are. Dependence on others can limit your talents.

2—Your feelings are uppermost and you are apt to turn others' opinions into personal affronts. This sensitivity can be very useful if you "tune" into people and see where they are. Cultivate a broader outlook on life and learn to be cooperative without being indecisive. Be thoughtful and consider the welfare of others as well as your own.

3—Social interaction frightens you and your reaction is to withdraw or become the loud overreactor. Each violent swing of the pendulum suggests that you are living in a personal construct without reality. Develop your sense of humor; try painting, dancing, writing or any artistic sort of self-expression that can bring out the real you.

4—This easy challenge is LAZINESS! However it can lead you into a rut where it is too much trouble to get out of that comfortable chair to answer the phone. Finish your cycles of activity and you will find your energy level rising. The other side of this challenge is rigidity. Learn patience and tolerance without becoming a slave.

5—This "freedom" number allows us to progress BUT it does not mean doing anything and everything we desire without paying attention to our responsibilities. There are laws of society and universe that tell us to use moderation, not overindulgence, in sex, drugs, alcohol or food. Organize your life. Recognize duties to family and friends.

6—This idealistic number may lead you into thinking that you have the best of all possible answers and belief systems. Your opinions can be dogmatic where personal relationships are at the crossroads. Do not impose your "perfection" on others. Give willingly of your time and knowledge without suppressing others' creativity. Turn "smug" into "hug."

7—This research and discovery number challenges you to become scientific and analytical. Heed your inner guidance. Develop a patience with existing conditions and make an effort to improve them. Do not stifle your spiritual nature. Your limitations are self-imposed. Cultivate faith in the justice of the general plan of things then seek to better it.

8—Wastefulness is the keyword for **8**. This can be brought about by carelessness or miserliness. A false sense of values, efficiency and judgements can become fetishes in the material world. Use your energies to cultivate good human relationships and avoid greed. Be guided by reason and not by avarice. Honor, glory, fame and money are okay if acquired in the right way.

9—This challenge is rare since it carries the lack of emotion and human compassion. It also means judging others and refusing to understand them because of an inflated ego. The time has come for this person to learn to love and empathize with others.

10—Here is NO or ALL challenges. Study all the NUMBERS above and see if you react to one. You have reached a point in your spiritual development where you can choose which challenge to release. Smooth the edges, learn and know the vibrations of the independence of **1**; the diplomat of **2**; the emotional thrust of **3**; the diligence of **4**; the expansion of **5**; the adjustment of **6**; the wisdom of **7**; the power of **8**; and the Universal Brotherhood of **9**.

If your CHALLENGES are the same as your DESTINY NUMBER, give it very close scrutiny.

NUMBERS

Every number can be expressed on three levels—POSITIVE—NEGATIVE—REPRESSIVE. This does not mean that a person is expressing on all three levels. You can evaluate yourself by observing:

1. How you react in certain situations.
2. What is your chronic emotional tone?
   Happy, grumpy, short-tempered, enthusiastic, fearful, bored, etc.?
3. Check how the interpretations listed below represent your over-all response to your daily grind.

POSITIVE	NEGATIVE	REPRESSIVE
Certain	Apathetic	Despotic
Enthusiastic	Unsure	Tyrannical
Definite	Antagonistic	Suppressive
Specific	Vacillating	Hostile
Searching	Non-feeling	Violent
Transforming	Covert	Stop Motions
Activating	Resentful	Hateful

This is the reason that people with the same numbers react differently to certain situations and differ in attitude towards themselves and others. You can choose which level you are now on and change your level if you wish to change yourself. You can also change your name or a few letters of your name to bring in the vibrations of your choice.

See our book on Name Analysis—POTENTIAL! This book gives you an in-depth analysis of your personality. It is soon to be available at book stores or can be ordered direct from the Rices.

Number **1**:
POSITIVE: Creative; optimistic; self-determined; creative mind through feeling; can reach a higher dimension of awareness when preceded by a **10**.
NEGATIVE: Indecisive; arrogant; fabricator.
REPRESSIVE: Tyrannical; hostile; ill-willed.

Libra Thru the Numbers

Number 2:
POSITIVE: Sensitive; rhythmic; patient; a lover; restful; a peacemaker; skilled; responsive to emotional appeal with love; protective.
NEGATIVE: Impatient; cowardly, overly sensitive.
REPRESSIVE: Mischievous; self-deluded; hostile.

Number 3:
POSITIVE: Communicative; entertaining; charming; can acquire knowledge from higher beings; inspirational; an intuitive counselor.
NEGATIVE: Conceited; exaggerating; dabbling but never really learning anything exactly; gossiping.
REPRESSIVE: Hypocritical; intolerant; jealous.

Number 4:
POSITIVE: Organizer; devoted to duty; orderly; loyal; able to heal etheric body by magnetism; works on higher levels; endures.
NEGATIVE: Inflexible; plodder; penurious; stiff; clumsy; rigid; argumentative.
REPRESSIVE: Hateful; suppressive; gets even.

Number 5:
POSITIVE: Adventurous; understanding; clever; knows the essence of life; creative mind on the mental level; traveler; creative healer.
NEGATIVE: Inconsistency; self-indulgence; sloppy; tasteless; inelegant.
REPRESSIVE: Perverted; afraid of change; indulgence in drink, food, dope; no sympathy.

Number 6:
POSITIVE: Harmonious; good judgement; love of home and family; balance; cosmic mother; self-realization; the doorway to higher mind through harmony.
NEGATIVE: Anxious; interfering; careless.
REPRESSIVE: Cynical; nasty; domestic tyranny.

Number 7:
POSITIVE: Analytical; refined; studious; capable of inner wisdom; symbolizes the bridge from the mundane to the esoteric; the mystic; able to heal spiritual gaps.

NEGATIVE: Confused; skeptical; humiliates others; aloof; a contender.
REPRESSIVE: Malicious; a cheat; suppressive to self and others.

Number **8**:
POSITIVE: Powerful; a leader; director; chief; dependable; primal energy; can open third eye; money maker; sees auras.
NEGATIVE: Intolerant; biased; scheming; love of power—fame—glory without humility; impatient.
REPRESSIVE: Bigoted; abusive; oppressive; unjust.

Number **9**:
POSITIVE: Compassionate; charitable; romantic; aware; involved with the brotherhood of man; successful; finisher; merciful; humane.
NEGATIVE: Selfish; unkind; scornful; stingy; unforgiving; indiscreet; inconsiderate.
REPRESSIVE: Bitter; morose; dissipated; immoral.

Number **11**: IDEALIST
POSITIVE: Idealistic; intuitive; cerebral; second sight; clairvoyant; perfection; spiritual; extrasensory perception; excellence; inner wisdom.
NEGATIVE: Fanatic; self-superiority; cynic; aimless; pragmatic; zealot.
REPRESSIVE: Dishonest; miserly; carnal; insolent.

Number **22**: PHYSICAL MASTERY
POSITIVE: Universal power on the physical level; financier; cultured person; international direction in government; physical mastery over self.
NEGATIVE: Inferiority complex; indifference; big talker—not doer; inflated ego.
REPRESSIVE: Evil; viciousness; crime on a large scale; black magic.

Number **33**: EMOTIONAL MASTERY
POSITIVE: The idealist with power to command or serve; leader who has emotions under control; constructive emotionally controlled ideas.
NEGATIVE: Erratic; useless; unemotional; not using his/her gifts of sensitivity to others.

REPRESSIVE: Power to work on other people's emotion to their detriment; riot leaders.

Number **44**: MENTAL MASTERY
POSITIVE: Universal builder with insight; can institute and assist world-wide reform for the good of mankind; can manifest his postulates.
NEGATIVE: Mental abilities used for confusion of worthwhile ideas; twists meanings of great statesmen and very able people for personal use.
REPRESSIVE: Crime through mental cruelty; uses mask of righteousness to do evil; psychotic.

Number **55**: LIFE ENERGY
POSITIVE: Abundant life; channels from higher dimensions with ease; brings light into existence; student of action; heals using life force.
NEGATIVE: Karma burdened with inaction on the right path; chooses to look backward and wallow in self-pity.
REPRESSIVE: Victim of life; in darkness; no path visible; withdraws; blames others.

Number **66**: LOVE ENERGY
POSITIVE: Self-realization through love; this love extends from self to others, knowing that one cannot love others unless one knows and recognizes the perfection of one's own soul.
NEGATIVE: Using love as a tool to enslave another; extreme selfishness and possessiveness; refusing love when time and person is correct.
REPRESSIVE: Seeing only the barriers to love; repressing loving attention to others; repressing the need to outpour cosmic love to others.

BIBLIOGRAPHY

Avery, K., *Numbers of Life*, Freeway Press
Bailey, A., *Esoteric Healing*, Lucis Pub. Co.
_____,*From Intellect to Intuition*, Lucis Pub. Co.
_____,*Initiation: Human and Solar*, Lucis Pub. Co.
_____,*Letters on Occult Meditation*, Lucis Pub. Co.
_____,*Problems of Humanity*, Lucis Pub. Co.
_____,*Telepathy*, Lucis Pub. Co.
Campbell, F., *Your Days are Numbered*, Gateway
Diegel, P., *Reincarnation and You*, Prism Pubs.
Fitzgerald, A., *Numbers for Lovers*, Manor Books
Johnson, V., & Wommack, T., *Secrets of Numbers*, Samuel Weiser, Inc.
Jordan, J., *Romance in Your Life*, DeVorss & Co.
_____,*Your Right Action Number*, DeVorss & Co.
Leek, S., *Magic of Numbers*, Collier-MacMillen, Pubs.
Long, M.F., *Growing into Light*, DeVorss & Co.
_____,*Huna Code in Religions*, DeVorss & Co.
_____,*Secret Science Behind Miracles*, DeVorss & Co.
_____,*Secret Science at Work*, DeVorss & Co.
_____,*Self Suggestion*, DeVorss & Co.
Lopez, V., *Numerology*, New American Library, Inc.
Rice, P. & V., *Potential! Name Analysis*, F.A.C.E.
_____,*Timing*, F.A.C.E.
_____,*Triadic Communication*, F.A.C.E.
_____,*Thru the Numbers*, Samuel Weiser, Inc. (a series for each zodiac sign)
Roquemore, K.K. *It's All in Your Numbers*, Harper & Row
Schure, E., *Pythagoras and the Delphic Mysteries*, Welby, R., & Health Research
Street, H., Taylor, A., *Numerology, its Facts and Secrets*, Wilshire Book Co.
Thommen, G. S., *Is this your Day?*, Crown Publishing Co.